Treasures of the Unconscious

by

Niall McGrath

Scotus
Press

Acknowledgements:

Acknowledgements are due to the editors of the following
journals, anthologies and other publications in which some of
these poems first appeared:

*Acumen, Awen Bard, Cyphers, Crannóg The Eildon Tree (Scotland),
Neon Highway, Skidrow Penthouse (USA), The Yellow Nib,
The South Carolina Review (USA), Ulla's Nib, Aesthetica,
The Ashville Poetry Review (USA), Poetry Ireland Review,
The Interpreter's House, Honeysuckle Honeyjuice, Never Bury Poetry,
Epoch, Quadrant (Australia), Northwords, Ulster Tatler*

Many thanks to Jack Harte, Pat Pidgeon, Colm McHugh,
Jim White and all at Scotus Press.

In memoriam,
John McGrath

First Published in Ireland by
Scotus Press
PO Box 9498
Dublin 6
www. scotuspress.com

Copyright © Niall McGrath 2009
ISBN: 978-0-9560966-0-9

Cover & Design: Pat Pidgeon
Layout: Colm McHugh
Set in 11/18pt. Garamond

Contents

Treasures of the Unconscious	11
Prophecy	12
Satanism in Suburbia	15
Diabolical	16
Shout!	18
Time Waster	19
On the Pull	20
Shut Up and Take It	21
A Stranger in the Court of Venus	23
Tusk	24
The Pilgrim	25
Rock G.O.D.	26
Love in a Northern Province	27
Botanic	29
Breakfast at Rankin's	31
Matchless Gifts	32
I Want To Be a Tree	33
Sunday Morning in the Garden of Eden	34
Vidcon	36
Capital Eye	37
Recollection	38
Death of a Motorcyclist	39
Urbane	40
An Ulster Nativity	41
Epic	42
Sex and Violence in Ballymena	43
Radio Walking	44
Catastrophe	45
A Phonecall from Heaven	46
Tha Call	47
Cod	48
Nuisance	49
Covenant	50
Plantation	51
Hoarding	52
Who Dares Wins	53

Bigger   54
The Enchantment of Mór   55
Freaks   57
Alarm   58
Here We Are Again   59
Caring   60
Automobile   61
2012   62
Lost World   68
The Proximity of Mars   69
Illumination   70
Out of Season   71
Child of the Sun   72
Fall Guy   74
To Michael S Begnal On Founding the
        James Liddy Society of America   76
The Prince of Outer Baldonia
        and the Pepsi-Cola Kid   77
Wanderlust   78
View From the Hill   82
The Front Gates   83
Burger and Milkshake   84
Chicken Soup   86
Fish 'n' Chips   88
Osso Buco – The Epitome of Fine Dining   90
Roadkill   91
Footnote to History   92
Down the Yard   94
Burden   97
Groundwork   98
Pallet   100
Honest Ulsterman   101
Groundkeepers   104
Genetic Engineering   105
On an Onion   106
A Farmhouse Kitchen in County Antrim   107
The Unrequited   109
The Accordionists   110

Elder	111
The Latest Crisis	112
Missing the Mark	113
Elegy for the Black Hill	114
Last Evening	115
Vision	116
Return to the Hill	117

Treasures Of The Unconscious

(i.m. Tommy Holmes)

The cortege drove from the church to the cemetery
past the end of the farm lane where he used to park,
wandering along banks in waders
most weekends for decades. In autumn dark
one evening at last season's close
the bailiff spied him still perched
on his stool after long hours, had to prise
him to his feet, as his eyes searched
the river valley with the same implacable stare
as his prey, whose eyes never shut,
I walk the banks he'll never see again,
a duckling dives beneath water, but
fails to surface; herons rise,
wings slapping air like pterodactyls;
swans glide amidst weeds' herbaceous scent;
still the weir vaporises as it spills.

Prophecy

Some things you can be sure of

I

Is it just a pong as you speed by the shore,
an unpleasant intrusion from the rendering plant
you pass as quickly as possible, ignorant
of the stench of manure and tallow in there?
The burger grease is on your smacking lips;
from the back, the kids stare across at smoke whisps.

II

A low sun burns as the day will always glow;
once, it was the day, or the day after
and those memories were real.
What validity is there now in such commemorations
when the grieving have themselves long since been mourned?
Fear not the passage of time,
for the time will come to pass
when saffron twilights suffuse with verdant hills and valleys
and all our days are naught but one.

III

God rest the learned gentlemen of yesteryear
who at odd species or down their trousers did peer;
who turned to nature, sex, chemistry and physics
to explain the mysteries of this and other cosmoses.
But as their bones melt to dust, the osmosis
of their conscious becomes the moot question.
Richard of York gave battle in vain.

IV

The tangs of fresh air radiate from the horizon,
smart in my throat like salt, entice
a surge of pleasure, reverberations
rippling from the whipping white blades that slice

on the emerald ridge, generating a static *frisson*
that moves my conscience to a trembling passion.
And the time comes when control resides
not in chimney stacks but remote hillsides.

V
Just how gay were those clay-spattered days
of so-called freedom, bare-breasted girls squirming on
scraggly-haired suitors? All out in the open,
anything goes, tattooed from neck to toes.
A generation of disobedient, self-serving brats,
mob rule in the streets after dark, that's
the legacy. That and the invisible regiments
of the pox-ridden shuffling to Outpatients.
Happier? In some ways maybe, some definitely.
But there are less tangible losses for the transgression virgin:
gone is the smut and innuendo of carry on,
the new repression to be overcome is amorality.

VI
Take pride in the dark sea if you dare,
recall the flashing blade and raging barrel if you care:
the innocent bleating to a death they do not understand,
teeth beaten from their bleeding heads,
knees sinking into sand as storm-swept beaches
ebb on the furious tide where stakes and crosses
are paraded like crude effigies to be burnt
by the ruthless, till tackled with swords of truth that will out;
the reversion, as fundamental as Iceland's conversion
from pagan feuds and blood bargains,
will see past miscomprehension
replaced by a more intimate darshan.

13

VII

Thick and sticky on the palate as wine,
regard the solemn faces in sepia pictures,
sneeze when the mustiness of old pages tickles
from between scuffed leather covers,
sweet to the memory as Parma violet:
these are inklings of some other experience
as distracting as déjà-vu; attracting the essence
of being. And what infinity of sons might it beget?
What offspring is this emanating from star-crossed lovers?
Ancient wisdom will be the news that prickles
hair on the back of the neck, its strictures
the new liberty, the preferred taste of the divine.

Satanism In Suburbia

A derelict, curving art deco shopping arcade,
skylights smashed, timbers tau-crossed on
      rubble-strewn floors,
black and white tiles arranged in geometric patterns
suggesting the Kabbalistic; rusting H-irons bare,
light flexes dangling as if execution chamber
cables; litter swirling in corners, glinting as dusk
casts gloom, as if it were the horns of goats, fangs of rats;
chilly gusts raise up the musty aroma of cats.

A sedan passes, its number plate reads 6-6-6;
a black hound growls sinisterly out at the world as
a party of Goths march in boots and black uniforms,
collars studded, faces streaked with paint like witchdoctors;
a drunk staggers by, bottle in hand, will lie the night
in that devilish grotto; will be found tomorrow
a stiff heap in rotting rags, a humming lord of flies.

Diabolical

On the plasma screen I witness scenes:
a group in camouflage robes giggle like youngsters
about to receive their First Communion,
their hair glittering like Roswell tinfoil;
behind them bodies fall past towerblock glass,
see how they cry like Edvard's pastel friend
as all crumbles into grey dust.
Even the pearl-pale cheeks of a girl with an earring
crinkle impasto, become arctic crags.
On a high ridge a Buddhist monk meditates to death,
mummifies his cause, the relief of his valley;
the salvation of impassive burghers whose ears are cocked
like terrorists' mercury tilt-switches, straining
to explode into action if the price is right
at the urging of golfing buddies, angel brokers –
Oh, what did the cleric say just then?
Eye off the ball; his hand on a hairless scrotum,
scratching, tickling, urging with a twisted finger
the innocent to submit under the fist of the fiery-eyed one.
Hand me a plate, garnished with mangetout and carrot,
the centrepiece the raw tent of chicken buttocks,
tear off legs, stuff its core to make it sweet,
chop it up like the jigsaw of a Flemish painting,
as dancing girls in leather bikinis stomp and whip,
gorging the masochist sprawling on the tabletop
handcuffed to Heaven's banister
calling out to those on either side of him:
Franz, write me a certificate, 40 days remission from purgatory,
Heironymous, draw me a picture on the plasma screen
of prisons in the desert or on a humid island
where a group in khaki titter as they snap
photos, posing like gods, imperial hunters who've bagged a kill,
bodies writhing in glorious ecstasy and agony

as they crack the whip for the damned.
Spotlight the body, as the mountains erupt;
as hail sweeps, cuts to the bone, stings eyes,
darkness surrounds; but the scene gradually focuses
on lichen-damp pumice walls - bobbing upstream
on a craft on automatic pilot, through the arch below the
        window,
pray refreshment lies somewhere beyond the flickering
        screen.

Shout!

If you break windows
you break more than windows:
you break hearts.

So what? you say,
wasn't your window broken first,
wasn't your heart broken first?

You were nice to people
and they didn't appreciate it,
often they took advantage.

You have to speak up, you say,
you have to be assertive —
if you want to be left in peace

you have to SHOUT!

Time Waster

Thinking of love, you don't waste any time:
you are late on your bike for our first date,
though seductive in skin-tight blue denim.

Your lonely hearts ad is written in rhyme,
speaks of romance, suggesting a soul-mate;
thinking of love, you don't waste any time.

You know what you want, being in your prime,
are businesslike, won't just leave it to Fate,
though seductive in skin-tight blue denim.

When I don't measure up – wham, blam, thanks ma'am –
you soon ditch me, find a sharper sweetheart;
thinking of love, you don't waste any time.

Your approach to relationships is a crime:
you hurt me bad, leave me seething with hate:
though seductive in skin-tight blue denim,
thinking of love, you don't waste any time.

On The Pull

Standing here
lined up like a steer
in a mart race
wonder is it my turn
and there's a look on your face
and I know I look cool
standing here
at the edge
of the dance floor
where you're boogying
with a gaggle of girls
short skirt, stilettos
as next to me your pal cadges
a drink from some lad
and off she goes
in a dark place, snogging
while you've been watching me
standing here
watching you
but when that guy starts posing
in front of you
you clasp around his neck
pull him close
over his shoulder
stick out your tongue at me
standing here

Shut Up And Take It

I
You've been on the piss
when some cutie passes a pill
and your mind's spinning
like a mirror ball,
you're able to hiss
'What's this?'
But the fun's just beginning,
don't wanna appear less
cool or miss a call
when he coughs 'Shut up and take it'.

II
You're rooted to the spot
at the desk in the empty office
when your line manager
has a quiet word,
does her duty,
informs you serious as a schoolmarm
Personnel want to stop the rot,
tackle absence
by being tougher,
hence this Note of Concern;
and you want to scream,
instead transcend the absurd
nonchalantly,
though your stomach pit burns,
you notice your increased heartbeat,
treasonous head pounding, 'Shut up and take it.'

III
Your limbs ache,
lungs heave,

throat gurgles involuntarily
as the Sergeant's in your face
bright with apoplexy
urging you to race,
and though you know it's fake
you are obedient
when he rants for you to deny
the pain and try,
to 'Shut up and take it'.

IV
It was a risky thing to do,
walk this way alone
this time of day or night,
no one noticing
when he grabbed you;
can't reach the cell phone,
squirming with fury
as the creep's fingers prod,
as he gives it to you good,
as he pants, 'Shut up and take it'.

A Stranger
In The Court Of Venus

When that young slut took interest in me,
being naïve, I couldn't believe my luck;
but it wasn't a case of *fine amour*, merely
a good old-fashioned Anglo-Norman fuck.
Next thing I knew, she had me before the beak
on a rape charge: a sly maintenance ploy.
So now, I sing a lullaby for the boy.

Tusk

There is a purple bruise upon your neck,
as if the blood, the life, were sucked
out of you; there is a deep mark
in its midst, a crater born of rage,
spit flying through teeth as snide remarks
are flung back and forth, doors slammed;
or ears cupped at doors, straining
to hear what's happening, what's said.

Lovebite. Love mark. Scar. Is pain.
Tearing the flesh. Not just physically –
a finger points to the temple, the heart,
shark's fang pendant at your throat.
Resentment grows, like a tumour,
a knot of worry; like an abortion -
a lump of tissue, protruding teeth, hair.
Desire thumping, spite pulsing like a drum.

The Pilgrim

He bounces in the cart
being taken home alone

through the twilit forest
across uncultivated heathland

he spies smoke-wisps ahead
hurries to pull on his trews

but the horse delivers him
to the peasants' cottages

before the citadel walls
they jeer at his nakedness

approaching the drawbridge
sentries ignore his entrance

as hooves irritate cobbles
he's observed from the keep

Rock G.O.D.

Firing flourbags from cars at Teddyboys
on arduous journeys back home from gigs
in the Sixties is how the pranks began.
Then disappearing socks or underpants,
chucking water over cameramen,
locking yourself in your dressing room before
a show, refusing to go on stage
until the contracted hour, regardless
of threatening riots; sending roadies
to pick a chick to order from the audience -
blonde and busty, just how you like groupies,
staying at a different hotel from the rest
of the lads, avoiding their drinking parties –
who do you think you are? You're just an aging
rockstar who thinks he's god. And so you are:
growing old disgracefully, prancing
about in black, scowling, smashing guitars
as if you were still a teen heartthrob;
yet I'll give you your due: they can't pick a chord
like you. The original, the best. Genius! Yob!

Love In A Northern Province

She sounded perfect in the lonely hearts column:
'Geraldine from Armagh, non-smoker, GSOH'.
The same professional bracket as myself;
so I called her up and delivered my pitch.
We met in a café, went to her place. Reaching for milk
in her fridge – racks of meat – I began to retch.

The first guy was sweet, but he hared off for some
inexplicable reason. Then, Conor from North Down
called my box number and we met on a windswept beach.
He was an academic, not in business, a bit of a clown
but cute. I dropped him when I found out he was a Prod –
I couldn't be seen with one of them in my home town.

After a false start I plucked up the courage to try again.
In the ad she sounded dead on: right age, religion
and so on. She called and seemed hoarse – had a cold,
she said. When I went to her place in Coleraine
she was a single mother, brain damaged after a car crash:
brave, caring, long-suffering – but too rough, common.

I thought Conor was okay, but he never called me back.
Just as well, probably one of these chancers
who just want to screw you and offer no commitment.
Then I arranged to meet Oran among disco dancers
at the local. It's a mixed thing but he's a hunk,
neither of us is bitter. He travels, inspects abattoirs.

This contact lark is the biz: I'm poking this wench
up in Coleraine, bonking one in Omagh, closer to home,
then see one in Enniskillen every weekend as well.
She's playing hard to get. Carmel, with the pert wee bum.
She's a civil servant in the city, comes back
to go to chapel and have Sunday lunch with her mum.

I met this Tyronie, Oran, at home, but he was just a lech;
I'm weary of small-town ways, despise rural Fermanagh.
I spend more time in Belfast now because I've met a lad
from Antrim. He amuses me, wines and dines me. Darragh
with the athletic bod. But it's not physical attraction
that unites us: we're meant to be, he's my *anam chara*.

Botanic

Sunday lunchtime in the university area
as lazy as a South-West summer weekend –
beer and chilli-con-carne at the Smugglers'
as light basks on cliffs and dunes.

It's autumn here and greyness pervades,
but this café full of trendy youngsters is stifling
for term's begun and ecstatic Freshers
are exercising newfound liberation.

The street's lined with cars, lampposts
chained up with bicycles; windows
drip condensation as red eyes peruse
the *Sunday Life* and *News of the Screws*.

The aging hippy who skulks to a corner
with his cravat, bifocals and *Observer*
Has a paternalistic smile to himself
for he briefly recalls his initiation:

late Sixties, the first boutiques brightening
post-war drabness and cappuccino bringing
a touch of exotic, continental sophistication
to this unlikely provincial backwater

so soon to be embroiled in a feud
that made international headlines
for a lost generation; those barricades
now a memory of his middle-age.

A black Singer sewing machine on one wall
like his mother used to rattle Saturday evenings
as he'd curl on the sofa before *Dr Who*'s whines;
next to it, a weighing block like his father had

in the outhouse, from which they dangled
the chickens and turkeys he'd plucked,
that squeezed their last warm cream
on his lap as stiffening feathers tore skin.

These inheritors wear peace casually, disturb
neighbours by jumping on car-roofs, break
trees in half, leave them to lie forlorn, wilting,
create nerve-shattering reports in night streets

which replace the vision-shaking explosions,
ear-drum numbing blast-waves they haven't known,
echo the siren screams, unquenchable panic
of the grieving.

           And if he stares over
his specs at them as they snort Madonnaesque
a little too loudly about their erotic exploits,
it's only a reflex prudery that assaults.

Here, Mexican, Chinese, Indian are *a-la-carte*,
for them are *passé*, lack the exquisite *frisson*
of *his* adolescence; but still he savours
recognising this brief, carefree moment.

Breakfast At Rankin's

Coffee aroma permeates sharp morning air,
brewing the darkness, invites the hungry
who have walked from car parks, ready for the office,
almost ready to face phonecalls, emails, in-trays.

Familiar smiles greet them, and displays of pastries,
sandwiches, fajitas, raspberry and almond scones,
a choice of blends, herbal, tea or frothy cappuccino,
warm, moist cake caresses the palate, creamy, buttery.

They drift from newspapers back out into the spate
of the streets, vaporising into the human current;
lipstick stains kiss cup rims, crumbs on plates bear witness
as waitresses clear tables, welcome other clients.

Matchless Gifts

(i.m. A C Bhaktivedanta Swami Prabhupada)

The Calcutta shopkeeper, with eight dollars
in his dhoti has two heart attacks in two days
as he is cargoed across the Atlantic by his friend;
disembarks in Boston, finding the way,
sets up stall in New York's Bowery,
Matchless Gifts on offer to the disillusioned
psychadelic generation with their crewcuts
or hippy long hair and scraggly beards.

They get high on mantras instead of rock,
groove to the sitar instead of electric guitars,
embrace his austere principles, forsaking
the false pleasures of the age, the free love,
cheap drugs, fuck-the-man Johnson and 'Nam
protests as Mom and Pop hold their heads
in their hands. If they could only realise
the sincerity they'd strike a light, too.

I Want To Be A Tree

('It's too hard being human, I want to be a tree!'
from 'Day' by Mary Herbert)

'It's too hard being human,
I want to be a tree!'
pronounces the hippy woman
with the long, wavy hair,
dancing on the spot
as if chanting for rain
to nourish her roots.
The oak groans in the cold wind,
branches bare, as frost
tortures every fold of bark
like the excruciating wrenches
of a rack. Sensing every strain
in this unreal world, wishing it were
the green man of myth, praying
for reincarnation in some more
pleasant form, able to tug
those roots from the damp earth
like legs, able to escape misery,
be freed from desire.
The callow youth, green as they come,
carries his treasure tucked inside
his anorak, so that he passes
unnoticed, at one with the street;
back home, ogles at photos
of the beautiful, gets high
on paper fantasies,
unreal relationships;
he does not realise it,
but he is becoming a tree.

Sunday Morning
In The Garden Of Eden

Fred Wilson is mowing his lawn, disturbing
the peace of everyone who's had a couple,
like Frank next door; whose beds are perturbing
thanks to all the weeds that rule.

Eva and Jules are heading to Yum-yums
for cappuccino and croissants and a dose of tabloids.
Mr Kirk, sixty-six, leers at their bums;
retires upstairs to cream his haemorrhoids.

Rocky Love is on his knees painting
flowerboxes either side of the front door;
he pauses to notice, opposite, a panting
Alasdair as he draws a curtain, chest bare:

Audrey is pumping a swollen breast
with a squeaking machine. At the shop later,
Billy admonishes Al for doing *that*
on the Sabbath: his righteous neighbour.

Billy returns to sit in the parlour
with his *Sunday Mail*, meanwhile Gwen
is preparing chicken, sneaks a gin
as hubby rants about today's social squalor.

Peter is in his loft conversion,
an amateur studio, getting to grips
with the intricacies of his latest creation,
re-oiling his model's nips.

His subject, single mum Sally, at thirty-eight,
is in the throes of an argument with her son,
who doesn't want to rise from his pit
for Sunday School now he's a surly teen.

She relents, so Luke wanders by the river,
his bitch loose, being full of reverie
eyes, ears and nose sparking with the electricity
rapt in the atmosphere generated by nature;

passes, unknowingly, Trudy and Eric
snuggled in the bushes, shooing away the dog
that tried to sniff his restrained dick,
rudely interrupted their surreptitious snog.

Jessie scampers with a momentary whine
from gorse clumps to rabbit holes,
destroys Luke's ecstasy when she mauls
a rag of rotting fur and bone.

Returning to the estate, Luke bobs on
as Fred mops his brow beneath a high sun,
merely nods when the old geezer speaks;
winces when the back door squeaks

and his mum calls out, while the TV titillates
with some reality show. Above the copse,
bells clang on the stillness
of another Sunday as the snake of time oscillates.

Vidcon

Desk, phone, microphone pad,
lack of lip synch, grainy
pixels, marble effect,
Turin-shroud-like décor.
This is true reality TV:
enthralled by the way she scratches
her knee, how he toys with his pen –
the drama of the mundane,
surreal when the man
on the screen speaks.

Capital Eye

Planes roar on uncharted courses
trailing clouds of glory as they soar
to unfathomable destinations, virtually
unnoticed by those in city streets.
We are suspended above ourselves
for a moment, have time-out to contemplate
a view across miles of buildings,
the rush and throng of traffic
and pedestrians frantic with the business
of work or love or domestic concern;
to slowly revolve in a capsule
on the awesome spindle
as if points at the radii of spokes
on a bicycle wheel, orbiting through time;
as rainbows whirl from the kernel and back again,
cycling to ground in drops of rain
from beneath the superstructure.

Recollection

(I recollect, therefore I am)

Sonny, are you there? his mother had called,
glancing through the panes of the scullery
window, admiring the green fields of home.
The boy was out behind the thatched cottage
in Malahide, checking the snare, had caught
something. His siblings had gathered around;
she peered over their heads, noticed wriggling,
murmured, *It's still alive* as the hare leapt.

Sonny, are you there? Jenny pleaded over
the phone from Northamptonshire, to the Leeds
pensioner she'd contacted, who could tell
the same tale about bleak hospital wards;
and when they met up, though their pulses throbbed
like breath beneath warm fur, their lips were still.

Death Of A Motorcyclist

There would be red faces, spittle flying,
fists raised at the graveside. His in-laws
were a rough crowd. But I held him, dying,
tissue caked beneath helmet, fractured jaw's
looseness startling under a sickle moon.
Blood tart on the air.
Threats in court, though judge and jury were aware
he'd strayed over the line,

clipped my headlight.
I'd had a shandy or two at the 'Port,
but I wasn't over the legal limit.
They were family, entitled to be mad,
yet weren't in the driver's seat
hearing thuds on the roof, groaning with him.

Urbane

There he goes, the dandy poet,
bohemian as they come, Oscar
himself! Thinks he's God's gift,
with his refined temper,

his dry wit, as suave as Shelley,
as elegant and affable as Byron,
as stylish as Pope in his formality,
as courteous and cultivated as Betjeman,

as conspicuous as Seamus. For all that, this bard
is so mannered he's a stultifying dullard.

An Ulster Nativity

"It is a wind which carries the seeds of life and the dust of
extinction… It is a winnowing wind. It is a bitter wind."
(Campbell McGrath, "Langdon, North Dakota")

I

March wind shivering in his heart
with flickering evenings of stars
and clouds of breath blowing against his shirt,
alone in the yard, squinting to bounce over bars
of a gate, as he hoists liths of straw
from mouths, moaning calves bucking
against him, hooves pressing on boots like claws,
always one with lips keenly finger-sucking.

II

And now, it's all only a December ache, flooding
on the breeze of nostalgia as he sniffs manure:
how he knelt before the hearth, parcels thudding
promisingly of Lego or some remote-controlled car
which never came. That one light on the plastic tree
winking: a dead brother's whispered glee.

Epic

I have witnessed the tail-end of extreme situations,
I am privileged to have shared time and space
with giants who bestrode nations
like classic gods, yet who have acted with grace,

dignity and integrity. They may be proud of all
that they have achieved; the generation who fought
a cosmic battle. And those who did not fall
made fields flourish, through austerity they wrought,

endured privation, built towns and cities,
engineered machines, nursed the sick,
transformed a tired, old sphere of spite and enmities
into a commonweal' of comfort and hope –

I marvel at efforts epic.

Sex And Violence In Ballymena

The sign of the cross, a fish, at your door
to ward off evildoers, as it rots.
The prostitute in fishnets
meets another midnight traveller
who's clean-cut and
expects the same; with drug-fuddled
tales of what the folks did to
or didn't do for her, she aims to shock
everyone including the lesbians strolling
to the cashpoint to collect their Giros.
The pair ignore her hysterics,
intent on their own worries, try to skirt
past a thug, who lashes out.
They flee, leaving the air tart
with the aroma of fresh blood. He smirks,
staggering into another bar;
They text a mate to warn her,
retreat to their flat to lick their wounds.

Radio Walking

I hear the distant mumble of music
rolling through high hedgerows
as I cycle along rippling lanes
with overhanging branches dripping
leaves down the back of my shirt,
summer evening warmth caressing
the hairs on my unsleeved arms.

Flitting specks ahead suddenly
fuse, bushes parting as if a sea
sliced by some vessel: two lads
with clown-like grins dodge
aside to let me pass, tyres
tsking their ingratitude as I force
brake pads, twist handlebars
to avoid the radio-walkers.
Two youths: one tall, brown-haired,
the other stocky, blond, red-faced
like a farmer's son – as we were
a generation ago, when we'd dander
these country roads of an evening,
dreaming of excitement while, as his mum
put it, *'Taking the radio for a walk'.*
Two silhouettes on the footbridge
above the motorway, waving
at blank faces in BMWs below
afraid of breeze blocks, radio
roaring with World Cup scores;
or, in the gloaming tarring field gates
black as the top ten beat out
its sensuous, sacred promises.

Catastrophe

(78 A.D., Pliny the Younger, on the Elder, as Vesuvius erupts)

I urge you to be cautious, seek safety with us,
but you are intent on marvelling at ash
vents, amazed by the terrible beauty
of pumice raining down. Boulders crash
nearby as if thrown by legionary catapults
and the eye-stinging, throat-clogging
fog of embers alights in our hair,
makes us retch during our blind jogging.

No gods obtund the admiral's last stand.
And I am left, glancing over a shoulder,
to record, who may be disbelieved for generations;
regardless of which, I will not stay this hand,
bear witness to stoicism on this shore,
suffer catastrophe to become celebration.

A Phonecall From Heaven

It's unplugged, yet the phone rings.
A familiar voice: I picture her face,
recall our youth: records play, she sings
along, teeth clamped in a brace.
That was before *he* became her friend.
Before he urged her to terminate
an innocent life; and, in that dark period,
that was the lesser shameful fate.

She asks, can I hear;
she tells me, *'It's okay here.*
There's nothing to fear.
And those behind...'
A buzzing; I'm earthbound.
I turn over, sleep sound.

Tha Call

(from the Scots-Gaelic of Roddy Gorman's Glaoch)

Ah phoned ye agin recently –
and, tha thing is, Ah wasn't tryin to irritate
ye in the slightest –
(In case ye believed Ah might be) –
on tha contrary –
Ah was enthralled to hang on, listened
to that jingle
on your ansmachine;
whose tune caused a confused
ringing in ma skull
and tha accompanying vocabulary
wasnae yet ma own.

Cod

(from the Scots-Gaelic of Roddy Gorman's Cur I gCeill*)*

Och ye strange, blethering beauty
yer without doubt
my favourite;
thanks agin
for letting me in
so I could get to know ye.

But just now
(damn it) I've to cod
that I need to hit the road
for the missis'll be
waiting at hame for me
and isn't it a fair bet she'll hae a knitted brow?

Nuisance

(from the Scots-Gaelic of Roddy Gorman's Toirmeasc)

You're a nuisance!
Drifting
in and out
skulking at the back of the house
without a care
as you linger
somewhere between this place /
and the next existence.

Covenant

Picture Carson in Edwardian frock coat
stooped at the table signing,
a quarter of a million men joining
him. And a quarter of a million
women had their own Declaration,
some using their blood as ink on the Covenant.

In the Public Records collection
I locate my grandmother's signature
and, beside it, her mother's.
It must've been a special day in Stranocum,
banners fluttering against azure
sky, a time of celebration.

Cassie was a stripling, of course;
knew nothing of what lay ahead:
how she'd be in O'Connell Street,
one of the bemused as Pearse
unscrolled *his* Declaration and read
and the world shuddered on its pivot.

How, at a dance, she'd meet
a freethinking lad, vow
to be his wife; learn
other shades of green;
and that pledges made in the heat
of the moment don't always ring true.

Plantation

The irony is, she was called Bess,
like the queen who sent them here
generations before. Behind this wall
she'd stroll safe from harm –

though in later years, aggrieved at rents,
McKnight let off his Blunderbuss
at the coach - his lordship was in Liverpool
the next night, never to return.

The irony is, they came for timber,
for they'd stripped their own shires,
yet here, their legacy was a copse of saplings.
A morning as chilly as their mausoleum,

I step through this *premier development;*
Bess's Moss, once bogland,
the roots of her planting have kept it drained.
Scots pine, sycamore, laurel

tower above five-bedroom homes
where the inheritors jog, mow lawns,
walk dogs where once only the loyal
were given space for their kirk.

Now, those who can afford to, choose to,
enjoy this arbour, this outpost
of the *desmense*, dwell within the lichened confines
of drystone marched territory.

Hoarding

You smile from a mobile billboard
parked and clamped in a lay-by,
have inspired the Connswater mall
to advertise with a similar blonde.
Your sandwiched posters proclaim:
one year gone but not forgotten and
your conscience must be killing you,
grieving for a sense of justice.

We drive on, this morning rush-hour
unmoved by a receding tragedy -
the rumours your body was dismembered,
dumped overboard in the Irish Sea.
Dark elements may have claimed the matter,
but deep waters still hoard your spirit.

Who Dares Wins

(The Boyne, 1690)

On the day before the battle
as opposing artillery pieces
rumble, thud and rattle,

with the enemy's field glasses
watching him from the far bank,
William of Orange ignores

the advice of his lower ranks –
his party dismounts to picnic
as volleys fly at their flank.

The sulphurous smoke is thick;
its smell begins to bed
like layers of city wall brick.

Meanwhile, over his royal head
shrapnel is lobbed back
and forth, as he breaks bread.

The bemused Jacobites crack
under the strain of his arrogance;
a cannon lurches back.

The Jacobite aim has been close –
Orange's shoulder has been injured;
a family feud has come to blows –

his father-in-law has drawn blood.
But this is only a foretaste:
tomorrow, the body-dammed river will flood.

Bigger

(i.m. Francis Joseph Bigger, 1863-1926)

This is Umgall not Roselawn,
surrounded by sheep and donkeys,
last resting place of farmers and journeymen.

Was it hoods who smashed
the tombstone in the Seventies,
or just some drunk local took the headstaggers?

His Crown and Shamrock pub
demonstrates largess: a pub embracing
both traditions, foreshadowing today's peace-making.

While others like Orr
are commemorated for the first time,
can rest in peace, undisturbed by the latest hothead,

Edwardian urns
and carved pilasters lie scattered here,
rusting railings now house a dump for branches and debris.

Antiquarian, scholar;
promoter of folk songs, music and Gaelic.
As I climb the stile, sunshine warms stone, mist rises.

The Enchantment Of Mór

Áed's daughter was a wee bit odd,
wouldn't leave the wattle-and-daub house.
Her head was plagued by a doomful voice:
Mór was sought by the kings of Ireland.

To escape the incessant torture within
in her derangement she climbed over the rampart
of her chieftain father's ringfort,
wandered till her skin was tanned by the sun.

She reached Cashel, where Fíngen ruled.
The locals let her earn her keep as a shepherd
watching the master's flock; but voices ordered
her to steal into his palace, lie where the fire blazed.

Affronted, Fíngen bellowed for her to be thrown out,
But his wife took pity on the hag and insisted
he sleep with Mór, otherwise his bed
would not see her own body again; the bright

jewels of the brooch she offered him did the trick.
So Mór was stripped of her rags, scrubbed
from hair to toe, the queen's servants perfumed
the stranger and decked her out in a purple cloak.

To his surprise, baring Mór's bosom
and exercised form, passion welled
in Fíngen; in sweet repose, he compelled
the peasant to tell him where she was from.

Her memory jogged, Mór was discovered
as the missing princess she was. In revelation,
presenting the transformed beauty to his woman
Fíngen informed that twinkle-eyed

madam that he was putting her away in favour
of the newfound mistress. As the ex packed
some things, a hesitant Mór approached,
expressed regret at the turn around

in their fortunes. 'Don't worry,' she smiled,
'Who's to say who's got the better part
of the swop? You've won Fíngen's heart
now he knows you're better bred.

I can see you're smitten already with Fíngen,
as I once was; you'll never leave him.
But don't fool yourself he shares the same whim,
you're anything more than a possession.'

Freaks

'Getting and spending we lay waste our powers,
Little we see in Nature that is ours...a sordid boon'
(Wordsworth)

He practises jumping in that awkward,
two year old way, shoulders hunched
like Pocoyo. Then giggles to "Mee-mee"
on the couch, climbs onto her knee, and pokes
a breast. She unclips her bra; he suckles.

'When's the wee one due?'
                                        'Next week.'
'Will you be sharing the night feeds?' 'She does that.'
'The trouble is,' the office sage squawks,
'when the other one wants some.'
Their Sixties logic prefers
uninterrupted sleep, so she can get back
to earning cash to buy formula
and pay nursery fees. Rather than *be* there.
He knows rightly their attitude
to attachment:
                    'Who could be bothered wi' tha'?'

Alarm

Glee turns to frenzy:
arms that lolled in bathwater
flail,
seize instinctively,
tiny hands grip my sleeve
as face flushes,
spittle flies,
bawling begins.

My arm's still beneath you,
you needn't fear; I support
you till my shirt's soaked through.
but I'm spooked by your stare:
for the first time we've seen
the frailty of trust.

Here We Are Again

A baby in the pram, asleep,
you aren't aware of this moment,
as we chat, or of your first – not a peep,
as when this midwife helped present.

A toddler when we meet
at the Mace again, you're more
interested in finding a treat
than the night your mother tore.

As a teenager, you slouch away,
pus-faced; but later query
who was that woman, anyway,
who's path crossed our's coincidentally?

Caring

You stare up at me with mute trust,
not realising we're separate entities;
our souls are entwined, as our bodies once were;
as your fingers are, now, with mine.
Your legs are too weak to hold your weight,
I clip your nails, pick the bogies
from your nose when you can't sneeze it clear;
make you burp as I massage your spine.

You scrunch up your face when I wipe your arse:
my cloth's too cold, perhaps you're embarrassed;
yet you are patient, - when your feed's late,
when your bed's wet, clothes have vomit
splattered down them, and around the room;
where your eyes stare, as if disengaging from here.

Automobile

Gotta burn that baby till there's exhaustion
gotta cruise that baby till all things fuse

see the vapours on the horizon
sniff the smog above the streets
hear the coughs of the tots
where has the clear view gone?

there's consequences to consult
as well as results
as well as shifting gear
there's righteous fear

just want to be
upwardly mobile
eyes smart too much to see
it's only for a little while

in the twinkling of your Ray-bans
you find yourself stranded on the arid highway
when all the juice has drained away

2012

I

A stench filters through the aircon
when I weave past the occasional vehicle
parked haphazardly at the roadside,
occupants still as manikins
Reality is stranger than fantasy:
tower blocks and offices,
malls and cathedrals
sprawling beyond this flyover
smoulder beneath
an Indian summer sky.
I detour into the city centre,
gape at the now domeless City Hall,
its white façade blackened;
shopfronts and winebars charred
like skulls on ritual pyres.
An emaciated looter zigzags
from a store with an armful
of cigarette cartons.
Fear weighs my foot down on the pedal -
I race from deserted streets
to the motorway,
Cream's *I Feel Free*
still pounding from the CD.

II

Toying with golden hair
she spies me in her rear-view mirror
through sunglasses
just as she did
in a rush hour traffic jam
not long ago
and I toyed with the notion
she was giving me the come on,

willing me to flash my lights,
signal for her to follow me
as in some corny pop video.
But now *I'm the only boy in the world*
and she is the only girl – almost.
Where's she from, and heading for?

III
The truck behind me is signalling.
Dare I trust him?
I cruise to a halt – no need to pull over
onto the hard shoulder,
there's no traffic other than us
and the occasional slavering feral dog.
I watch as the driver descends from the cab,
strolls towards me cradling a shotgun.
He's wearing a creased suit, tie askew.
I manoeuvre the car so I can speak to him
through the window, but I'm ready
to floor it if need be.

IV
'Surely you know it's not safe to travel alone?'
Her expression gives it away.
'Where have you been this past week?'
'At my mother's holiday cottage at Murlough.'
'No power?'
            'We've got a turbine now,
but I don't bother with TV or radio.
I like to escape the rat race,
now that I've overcome my demons,
and avoid rehab again,
by spending my days walking along the beach

or painting and reading.'
'Didn't you try to phone home?'
'My mobile's died. *What's* going on?'
I try my best to explain
as the satellite channel did in the last few hours
before power stations shut themselves down
and communications networks failed.
Which came first, bio-warfare pandemic
or random missiles?
'If you want, you're welcome to join
our community.' I tell her how
our first priority, as the hours of electricity
and communications ebbed, was to secure dairies
and organise a milking rota,
while phoning madly to beckon friends
to our country *demesne*;
desperately seeking family like my niece,
17, no driving licence or firearm,
braving 300 miles of now bandit-lurking
country to reach us, to collapse
into our arms in silence;
taking trucks, like this trip of mine,
scavenging supermarket storerooms
and shelves for the new essentials:
candles, matches, tins, flour, yeast,
DIY warehouses for tools,
garden centres for vegetable seeds,
agricultural merchants and isolated outhouses
for sacks of potatoes, wheat, grass seed.
For the new present is self-sufficiency,
if we can survive the first few years:
hook up to generators till stocks of fuel dwindle,
scour empty land for solar panels, turbines,
dig wells, hone skills to allow some to specialise

so that a power grid can be rationed,
before expanding roots and encroaching tendrils
do irreversible damage.

V
It's all too much to take in.
I decline the offer of sanctuary,
head homewards,
hoping to find *someone*.
The juggernaut lolls behind
till we reach the turn off
for the last suburban junction.
Squads of sports cars swarm around me,
force me to halt.
I noticed the truck in my rearview mirror
hissing to a standstill.
An unshaven, tattooed oik
commandeers my passenger seat,
jabs a rifle at my neck, grunts an order.
I follow their convoy, notice the truck
encircled behind also being
herded towards their compound.
They've erected ridge fencing
around a housing estate.
Bonfires leap on waste ground.
I'm dragged from my car
to witness them haul open
container doors.
Shots echo; rounds zing.
Bottles explode in flames
like grenades as armed lads
surge from the lorry.
I duck back into my car,
drive bent over, barely able

to see over the dashboard,
back to the motorway.

VI

Our lot have the upper hand,
so I hare after her,
once again flash hazards, beep,
overtake till she sees who it is.
As the lone car indicates my heart races,
I lift a foot from the accelerator;
praying for amity, pining for home.
I try to justify what we've just done:
how we'd heard about that tribe
on the grapevine, where the brutes
mug every passing male and enslave the females,
raid outlying communities rather than
sweat to produce their own sustenance,
how it'll be some time before representatives meet
to agree rules, policing, judgement.
And while there may be survival
for future generations, there will never be
any complete restoration, any return
to the orgy of over-indulgence
we once took as the norm.

VII

It's getting late. He promises someone
will accompany me tomorrow
to help me find and bury my folks,
salvage some keepsakes if I decide
to make their community my new home.
Two women kindly fill a bath for me.
As I'm towelling myself in the room,

66

I overhear them chatting:
'Will she be any use to us?
Trained as a manager in Daddy's company,
but can she cook, sew, knit,
plant seeds, weed, thin carrots and turnips,
pull her weight?'
'Aye, she confessed
she was a party animal.
Is our community the type she's seeking?'
'Is she too headstrong to contemplate
the need for a reversion,
such as us women of a certain age
being needed for the rebirthing the species?'
And it's now that an overwhelming sense
of epiphany sweeps through me,
that I *know* –
despite all our ineffable loss -
I am where I should be.

Lost World

You don't have to penetrate the centre of the earth
or delve beneath northern seas to convince me
there are lost worlds to discover. A soccer pitch
is 700,000 years: take one step, you stride past
centuries - the Romans, Iron and Bronze Ages even -
arrive at the Stone Age. From there to the end of time
(or should that be the beginning?) you meet but a few
scattered bones that you could fit in a shoebox.

So don't sound so sure when referring to scientific
evidence. You await those fateful 'missing links'
that have never been found. Evolution, adaptation, moves
in mysterious ways, can bound in one generation.
You're supposed to possess an open mind, but none
are so blind as those who will not see what little proves.

The Proximity Of Mars

(26th August 2003)

I hadn't seen these friends for two years;
the kid was in her womb at our wedding;
he bounced on his daddy's belly, wanting
to go to the planetarium to see Mars.

I stared out the back window as mother
chatted on the phone; they'd been out
for a look at the Heavens, because the paper
said today was the day and it was a clear night.

We shivered in the dark garden as we searched
for that orange blob in the sky, separating
Capricorn and Pisces; the neighbours deliberating
which bright light it was as constellations marched.

I went up the road beyond the cast of neon
with the binoculars but found my vision
better with the naked eye; passed by a lichen-
covered stone that meant more to other humans.

Just as this unique occasion almost drew
strangers together – Hale Bopp, Halley's Comet,
the total eclipse, we've witnessed all these – yet,
how much more they knew.

Illumination

Suspended particles in vacuum,
taut density burgeons in darkness; this tomb
houses the dead – a flask, contains what matters.
Stuffy. Static. Reaching crisis, gutters,
enflames, like striking a match, spontaneous
combustion, ignites, lightning blazing, explodes,
a roar still heard through satellite dishes.
And that condensation's blinding flashes
still burn, its resultant sparks alight,
like fireworks in the vast emptiness of night.
The dust and debris have yet to settle, collide,
congeal, a billion cosmic battles subside
as the blast gradually decelerates,
its force loses pace, stretched dissipates,
is sucked back on itself, returns to the source -
a heavenly chariot of ancient Norse
sagas – until fusion draws all the light
so tight into that womb once more black night
reigns supreme. And the process begins again,
and life gives birth to life, illumination
is born from utter darkness. We can know
it if we peer carefully enough: the glow
of reality, endless, repetitive,
expressed in the symmetry of all things alive.

Out Of Season

Will there be wildflowers at the backs of hedges
and mosses yellowing underfoot,
brown silt drying to cracking at the edges
of sheughs as summer's heat
intensifies; will there be a wasp
flitting down your neck, out through your shirtfront,
snowflakes gusting through tractor doors
as you tedd swards of hay; will prints
taken by American tourists capture
you silhouetted against orange sunsets
pitchforking bales high onto the trailerload
in the field passed by future Presidents?
Will you stand expressionless, greatcoated,
dog by your side, wince, gasp?

Child Of The Sun

(i.m. Fred Ellis Mayhew Jr, 1916-44)

I fell in France during the Normandy campaign, lay
in a field like Rimbaud's sleeping trooper, died – as I lived - in
    obscurity:
the facts are unclear. Had I an accident? A hand on my chest,
    motionless,
perhaps, smiling like a sick child? Or blown to bits? That great
    war
during which I was born saw 70% of casualties caused
by artillery – and so it was I was assigned to a Howitzer
    battalion.
Not for me the first heroic dash across the beaches, I followed
    behind,
lobbing shells to soften up the enemy. *I wander all night*
and day in my vision, open my eyes over the staring eyes
of sleepers, the bloody, pale or blue features of twisted corpses,
observe the gashed bodies of Americans on the battlefields
    of Europe,
so many ordinary Joes. Night pervades, enfolds them,
dew glistening with their drying fluids on leaves of foreign
    grass.
Jude, I could be called, though I'm not Jewish, just another
    WASP.
A man from Spokane – the only famous one was Bing Crosby.
Even that's not true: I moved to Clackamas as a child,
when Mam found herself a new man.
All you can know about me is facts from the Internet:
census details, military records. A search unearthed the Purple
    Heart
with my name engraved on the back. You'd imagined me some
    vet injured,
who sold it in a pique, or because he was hard-up.
The truth is, as in everything to do with me, undramatic:

some family member got rid of the thing after I'd gone.
Letters to veterans' associations bring
no anecdotes from old buddies to brighten my memorial.
Yet, I must thank you for thinking I am hero, of sorts,
to be celebrated as much as any Audie Murphy,
not least because I died on the Fourth of July.

Fall Guy

You seem so serene and composed
as you descend headfirst,
go down in history for your ten seconds,
one leg cocked like an Irish dancer.
We don't like to look,
wish to respect your privacy
at this most private of moments,
yet peer through parted fingers
from the sidewalk
in morbid fascination.
We revolt at the thought
of anyone not blown clear
or falling:
to jump is the ultimate humiliation,
the greatest sin.
Yet let us cling for a moment
to the burning sills by our fingertips,
let our backs scorch with the furnace-blast
of this towering inferno
like a chimney going up in smoke,
let our throats rasp, lungs heave
with the acrid fumes
and then not know the desperation
rather than merely turn our heads
in revulsion at the sound
of bodies thwocking to the ground
like bags of cement.
One still is not enough to convey
your predicament: though we know
your graceful drifting from on high,
other shots snap you contorting,
arms outstretched like a tau-cross,
as the leader flailed this morning;

and where is the voice, like that
of the father, to resolve that
this will not stand,
that the twin towers will stand again,
that Masada shall not fall again?
Each anniversary, twin columns of light
mark the spot, stand sentry like ghosts;
birds circle, a silent flypast,
lost souls saluting – as we must salute you,
for *all* the victims were innocent.
And yours was the most quintessentially human death
      of all,
you, who perished spiritedly, proudly as you did,
seized a last moment of self-control
rather than submit to some other destiny,
played the last act according to your own script
as if directing from the gods;
in doing so at one and the same time
embracing and snubbing a most unjust deed.

To Michael S.Begnal Founding The
James Liddy Society Of America

You may, said Oscar Wilde to the dandy culchie bard,
you may sing of Dionysus,
The cock oftimes crows in Wexford
or Wisconsin. The dandy culchie bard
kept stuffing the cock into his whiskey tumbler. *Lovely,*
cried Oscar, Go feast with panthers!

I am a poet,
the dandy culchie bard remarked to Oscar,
I will recline in the light with my obscure lines.

The Prince Of Outer Baldonia
and The Pepsi-Cola Kid

In the fourteenth year of treason,
according to Saint Joe,
the Reds in the State Department
were ignored as he sought quick dough:

the bank's examiners rejected
a note for twenty grand
although it was signed by Arundel,
who owned the fabled island

off Canada's coast, Outer Baldonia.
The Senator got sugar
rationing scrapped for Pepsi-Cola's
lobbyist and speculator.

A pyrrhic victory for the would-be Tailgunner-
turned-politician, self-publicist
who would attack the Army to score
cheap points, unwitting puppet

of a Commi who conned him into
alleging torture and murder
at Malmédy. All lies, innuendo:
condemnation his own career.

Wanderlust

Contemplating a photograph of my mother in the arms of a
    man other than my father,
I'm reminded of D H Lawrence's *The Rainbow*: the
transformation from a previous generation's relative innocence,
    to our own more jaded circumstances.
It is in a Brooklyn bar she is being cuddled, bright booze posters
on the walls, all glitz and glamour, shiny dress, rich hairstyle – its
    not just the shock of seeing
her face so young, skin so fresh, eyes sparkling like mirrorballs –
can this trendy young thing be the same person who squints over
bifocals in a worn-armed sofa in a drab farmhouse living room
    in rural Ulster?
Other pictures of happy days in the Big Apple,
all smiles amidst the pristine snow of some quaint Eisenhower
Christmas; a series of fellow nurses bagging their perfect man –
church steps snaps – it took her father's cancer and a return
    home before mum would take
an old flame, dad – the one she left behind some years before –
    for a husband.
Of course, there is the family trait to take into consideration
    – the Norse wanderlust
that saw her brother, Uncle Willie, to Dunkirk and back, forced-
    march up through Italy,
then tent out in the Australian bush after a ten pound voyage.
The same wanderlust, perhaps, we all share – if not actually
    going for it,
then at least dreaming about those palm-fringed tropical islands
I visited in my youth – which turned out to be too hot, too
    sandy, too insect-ridden.
The older the race, the more genetic mutations – Africa, experts
    say, is the cradle
of humankind (at least one hundred and fifty thousand
    years ago – several thousand generations).

The rest of us in the world lack Africa's diversity –
unless we resort to hybrid vigour, to keep the species strong.
What made us – hominids - special? Polar ice caps forming
    with the first big
freeze-ups, hence drought in the savanna, driving folk in
    search of – survival? –
hence they preferred to outwit extinction in cold northern
    countries, like ours.
Always remembering the glaciers reached Mayo, Ulster's
    border, but not Dublin
and the pale. What goes around comes around? How far
    back *does* the story go?
They say *homo robustus* didn't make it because a diet of nuts
    (for protein) and berries
was just too difficult to sustain – true, he didn't have great
technology, great organisation; yet some experts talk as if as
    if vegetarianism were a crime.
Even *homo erectus*, who stretched to six feet in height, with a
brain half the size of ours, struggled – not a frog in the
    throat, but a lack of the muscle
development that any two year old *sapiens* achieves – so that
    they can speak –
rather than his mere baby talk - more than the chitterings
    of a chimp, but not enough.
Some say *homo erectus* and the *Neanderthals* stimulated
evolution toward the consummate human being due to
their consuming meat – all that protein encouraging soft
tissue development in the brain, grey cells pumped up by
    blood.
Yet the same evidence shows how difficult it was for early
    man to hunt game;
and what about our fellow carnivores, tigers and other
    species – where are the

schools and hospitals they've built for any pride? If we turn
    to ancient tomes,
some tell of Rama – two million years ago – consorting with
    the half-ape-man,
Hanuman; how they had a civilised existence then; how it was
cow's milk that sustained the young, helped nurture them, as
    agriculture meant people
could focus on spiritual and intellectual development, not just
    mere survival.
Now they say genetically we are close to the mouse; just as
    rats and humans are
the only two species to slaughter their own species wholesale.
Caligula was a wretched tyrant and pervert: assassinated,
legionnaires half-burned his body in a pit – images of Hitler -
    then left his remains to rot in a shallow grave.
They say Caligula's ghost haunted the imperial palace until his
sisters retrieved his bones and performed a proper burial –
even the worst of souls requires some last
semblance of dignity, some acknowledgement of the essence
    that resides in the heart.
The heart – the seat of the soul, to the ancients. I watch *John Q*
and wonder how heart transplant affects that theory – a
    surgeon flicks a muscle, it beats again –
may as well say the immaterial soul is recalled to its host
    material body. My mother, matron
and theatre sister, said there was a 21 gram loss of body
    weight or density
at the point of death – that prompts so many physicians and
    scientists to faith.
Maybe some day bones will be unearthed than will speak
    volumes about our origins.
I won't be surprised if we never know the true story – just as
    I know I'll never know

all there is to know about my mother's sojourn in the States.
     And as for my father?
I once asked him what did he do all those years from
     adolescence to marriage
at age thirty-eight – with a twinkle in his eye he said, 'I'd the
     time of my life!'

View From The Hill

Snow drifts high, leaves an air pocket in a gully
where ewes cling by the hooves to life;
father carts one half-dead trailer-load home.
When the thaw comes, scores of ribcages
burn white on stiff grass. Summertime, he lies
by the back fence, peers with binoculars
across Anderson's farm to where black
barrage balloons bob over parliament buildings.

In an office block in the estate, his suited son
weeds Thirties files: petitions from farmers
who've defaulted on annuities, pleading with the minister
not to confiscate their smallholdings; pauses to peer
across at that other hill, before returning home
to tred the marches in wellies with the collie.

The Front Gates

Traffic lights streak scarlet and white in rain,
pedestrians rush across the street as amber flashes;
buses' brakes hiss, taxi signs beam like sun-rays;
shop windows blaze, offer occasional frocks,
choc boxes, electronic games
and gadgets, DVDs and CDs.
Cars brake on cobbled ground at the end
of Royal Avenue, pausing in the arcing
gateway of City Hall – the huge railings closed,
though a security guard watches for authentic
VIPs – as shoppers flop into backseats,
click in safety belts; are whisked away
towards their destinations, individual dwellings –
their time before the grand white building brief.

Burger And Milkshake

Daisy's plucked from her mother's teat
before she even gets a suck of colostrum,
is herded into a drylot, devoid of grass,
reared on feed pellets. No age, her tail's
wheeked off, no anaesthesia, though
they do jab her head before gorging
out her horn buds with a hot iron.

Her four stomachs have evolved to digest
grass's roughage, but she's stuffed with grain
till her metabolism riots and she stumbles lame.
She's induced to produce a calf a year,
which in turn is snatched from her
so machines can suck the milk from her sore
udder, inflamed with mastitis, seeping pus.
She should live over twenty years, but
after four this forced production renders her
spent. Carted to the stinking factory,
she waddles in file, skittering forward
when prodded; the guy with air-gun
is supposed to stun her with a bolt
to the forehead, but four shots and still
Daisy's standing bellowing in distress,
But the line doesn't stop – the chain
round her hind leg hauls her weight up,
image of subjection, till the sticker
cuts her throat, attaches a hose she bleeds into
to keep the place clean.
Daisy's still conscious when others in aprons
nick ankles and shred the hide, reveal
the glistening definition of muscle,
slit her chest and belly, begin
ripping organs, spilling intestines

into skips beneath them.
Next thing you know, Daisy's before you,
in cardboard punnet and polystyrene cup
on that Formica table in the burger joint,
reassembled as burger and milkshake,
yummy.

Chicken Soup

Warm aroma, inviting tan colour,
chunky cubes of flesh to bite into...
mass of feather-fluff within Perspex,
plucked from the crowded incubator,
she'll never see sky, grass, trees,
spends all her days in a wire cage –
no room to rustle her wings,
dust bath, scratch, dance freely–
tumbling over and being crawled over by
a crowd of others. Who peck;
like sparring prison inmates;
and she pecks back,
until part of her beak's cut off
so she can no longer preen.
Her brothers are taken away –
they don't share her ability
to produce eggs, so a couple are gassed,
though one's conscious when they're tossed
into the crusher, ground up alive;
the other, suffocated, joins them.
Our heroine paces the cage, anxious
to find a spot to nest, never will.
She must squat on a wire floor,
lay her eggs amidst the cage's bustle.
Lack of exercise has left her bones weak,
collisions with mates cause breaks.
Sometimes, there's no water for days,
which artificially causes moulting –
the cycle's speeded up, she lays
far more than is natural. When it takes
its toll and no more eggs appear,
she's jammed into a crate with other
rejects, batters around inside on truck

and trolley till a few more bones break.
She's shackled alongside her mates
on a conveyor belt, hanging upside down;
no laws insist she be anaesthetised;
an automated knife slices off her mate's head,
but it only catches her a glance,
chops a whack off her crown.
The last thing she sees is the cleaver
in the latex glove as it comes down
to render her into fillets and wings.
The guy handling her with chain mail glove
is on carcass number sixty-six of ninety
per minute – for low pay, but if he slacks
he's out all the same, so he doesn't
nip off for a comfort break,
pisses on the line; his urine
mingling about the cuts of meat
with the hen's own faeces
that sprayed out in her final throes.
All the same, her body's been so damaged
during her brief life it's not fit for
roasting, only pies and the like.
Like chicken soup.
Warm aroma, inviting tan colour,
Chunky cubes of flesh to bite into...

Fish 'n' Chips

The nets stretch for miles, how could we avoid them?
Gills caught in the mesh, after twenty-four hours
a sense of drifting: we're dragged and thumped
against rocks, underwater debris, then when hauled
in a rubber-gloved hand squeezes my belly, but no
he can't get me forward so what does he care? He rips
me backwards, gills torn at each side. Raw and sore,
I watch fellow cod thrown back in – too small.
Already all-but dead. Birds peck what life's left
out of them as they float, exhausted, shocked, pained.
I almost pass out when I land with a clang in a metal bin.
My eyes bulge, it feels like they'll explode –
the pressure change dizzys me. Mates bang into me
as they're thrown in on top. Someone thrashes
for a while; many others puke up their guts.
Stench of salt and vomit as blood and sick seep.
A breeze on my scales, I'm lifted skyward –
the glinting blade slits my gill-arches,
I'm discarded into another bin, to gasp and bleed
till my belly's split, innards spilt, beheaded.
My head and viscera, at least, are returned
to the ocean, along with the quarter of all
they caught, who weren't the right species
who weren't, like me, a *quare cod.*

A spray of mist hissing from booms
behind the tractor as it bounces over drills;
a spray of pellets scattering like hail
from the spreader behind the tractor
as the artificial's applied. The tubers will
swell, burgeon in the soil, into fat,
ripe chippers, ready to dip in lashings
of lard, to fry in the greasy spoon

alongside the doughy mush of batter-
encrusted cod flesh, stripped of scales
and bones, innards, head and tail,
as if it never had a life of its own,
swimming freely beneath the waves,
in its own world, master of its own soul.

Osso Buco
- The Epitome Of Fine Dining

Ingredients: Serves: 6
4 x 1-inch veal shanks   1 large onion, finely chopped
    (2 ¾ pounds)   1 medium carrot, grated
2 ribs celery, sliced   1 can of tomatoes, crushed
2 cloves garlic, minced   ½ cup white wine
1 cup beef broth   4 sprigs fresh thyme, crumbled
2 strips lemon zest   2½ cups dried angel hair pasta
¼ teaspoon salt
3 tblspns snipped fresh parsley
pre-heat broiler, sprayed with olive oil

Using 100% milk-fed Veal

Solitary crates, too small to allow
each scrawny calf to turn round
or stretch out to sleep naturally;
denied water and solid food,
fed only with a formula-milk replacement
deficient in iron so that the meat
is lean, pale, enough to make the gourmet
water at the mouth. Regardless
of the bawing, neurotic twitching,
restless blattering in sudden, brief spasms
of desire to escape, though they've never
known the green pastures some untapped
recognition urges these calves to crave.
Of course, the blessing is they only have
to stick it for a few months,
till they get the chop.

'It is difficult to defend the routine imposition
of unnecessary harm.' David deGrazia

90

Road Kill

A pad down the bank from the hedge
leads my gaze to where this carcass lies;
only the fox's bones remain,
once verge grass grew through rotted flesh;
to be crushed into muck by a tractor's tyre
as the councilman mowed April growth.

Already a bloody splodge
on tarmac, the hedgehog's
bristles glint in spring's
clarity; uninteresting.

You'd imagine the pigeon would fly out of the way;
if I'd known, I'd have honked the horn, not just driven on.
It waddled, its back turned, oblivious to danger.
When the grille struck its head - an eruption of feathers.

Footnote To History

'Like dolmens round my childhood, the old people'
                                    (Montague)

Like some character mentioned in passing in an ancient legend
who no doubt was alive to original hearers of the epic,
I turned musty pages to read your father's name, his tragic
death in the first Troubles, victim of a raid.

Things went too far, then. And also on a winter's day,
flurries of snow making your hand red,
Feckin' oul' bitch! of a cow wouldn't stand
at peace, would fret and buck and sway

in the chute of the cattle crush by the shed.
Drips plinking off the rusty gutter
as you would check injection sites, mutter
swelling readings from callipers for me to record.

The last time I was keeping a beast at bay
for you, you were chatting and mentioned
something and I scowled, *Yes* ; and the way
it came out you might've thought me rude –

patronising even, partisan in emphasis even,
though all it was was merely my own embarrassment
about it, wanting to avoid the subject.
Many times after that I hoped we'd meet again

and I'd get the chance if not to apologise or set
the record straight, at least to say something
that might assuage past sharpness of tongue,
show some sign of fraternity with a vet

who endured cold climates, offered often unthanked
ministrations. Some did not respect you out of prejudice,

whether or not they knew the sorrow that stalked
your youth; but, please, do not count me thence.

These characters in ancient sagas, these folk who embody
my childhood, to many they may be mere words on a page,
but to me none are footnotes to history,
all, like you, are heroes for every age.

Down The Yard

Where human weakness has come short,
Or frailty stept aside,
Do Thou, All-Good - for such Thou art -
In shades of darkness hide.
  (from A Prayer In The Prospect of Death *by Robert Burns)*

Here is the meal house, inside the door
down the step the grain bruiser
Willie John installed with my father,
stone blocks cemented to the floor
as a plinth on which it thunders,
barley slipping through the funnel
from the 8x4s above; those panels
John and I nailed down one wet summer,
after the choking when, with claw hammer,
I smashed rotten floorboards into lighters.

And here is that loft that once boasted
hessian bags of beer-humming roasted
kernels, sieving into the funnel, deafened
by the clatter of the tractor-driven belt;
above, on the grimy ceiling the imprint
of candle-soot, where Hugh Tully burnt
his initials the time he was an itinerant
labourer sleeping up here, each half-year
standing in Antrim's market square
hoping to be taken on by some farmer.

And here is the pig house where now broken
bulbed infra-red lamps once glowed, wooden
pallets and straw to warm sow and farrow,
one pen houses instead a load of blocks in a barrow,
lately white feathers caught on cobwebs

after chickens, that had pried with their nebs,
had their necks pulled, backs plucked,
and the box where Fly lay now tucked
aside, unused, by the miscellaneous implements
stored for a mate who repairs industrial equipment.

And this is the byre; that John, Neil and I
rebuilt, feeding a cement mixer its gruel of dry
sand and cement, quenching its thirst with water
and a dash of Fairy Liquid till it drooled mortar;
the byre where Da and I scale the ladder
to clean dirt from the ballcock washer,
where the fertilizer spinner rests caked in oil,
the power-hose hibernates, its cable coil
tripping up the unwary as they head for the huge
bale of sheep-wool that never made it to the gauge.

And this is the stable: a pokey wee shed now,
where you'll find an orphaned calf or sick cow
quarantined, bawing behind the black-tinned gate,
that lay open against the wall the time Mummy caught
Da, barrowful of manure in his rolled-up sleeved arms,
         to tell him,
breathlessly, how the hospital were on the phone,
Willie John was gone.

Here is the long shed, the front wall of which collapsed
under the weight of snow on the slates, like a lapsed
devotee it turned its back on duty, yet didn't harm
a single beast inside. The long shed in our farm
yard that John Moore couldn't finish patching up due to
his first coronary, so the other John oversaw the new
form's appearance from the rubble strewn over the pile
of gravel tipped against that shed's front wall.

Here is the dwelling house, abandoned by each generation
of tenants, re-inhabited despite several condemnations,
where Joe lay clutching blankets over his head
one dark night when a storm raged
and tree branches scraped the skylight pane
like the fingernails of a demon trying to get in.

And here, this metal gatepost we now tie
the aluminium ten-footer to, I
was repainting this the time Geordie and Ivan
were separating beasts in the arch-roofed barn
and I was feared the toothless one might've tossed
a fag-butt into tinder-dry hay, so I accosted
them, instinctively gave lip the way the old man
or Willie John would've done,
and realised I'd reached another stage of maturity,
here, down the yard, where profundity
resides in obscurity,
nostalgia mingles among the ordinary.

Burden

A salutary lesson, in stoicism,
sense, whatever, as I lay beneath
the bale of hay on the dusty silo
black plastic coversheet in toddler
weakness, unable to lift the heavy
burden off my chest, hands and cheeks
scratched by rough stalk-ends,
throat and chest troubled by mustiness
as I struggled to free myself.
It was Uncle Alan, for all his schitzo
darkness, who had pity in his eyes
as well as an unlit fag behind his ear
going soggy as the sweat dripped
beneath corrugated tin roof,
when he raised the bale from
the yapping boy who wanted to be
grown up before his time
but only got in the way.
How much time passes? Not much
till the scene changes from that summertime:
Uncle Alan has succumbed to the black tar
in his lungs, Dad crippled by the tightness
in his heart – it's this teenager who carries
bales from barn to shed, invoices stuffed
into pockets, rubber boots split where
I've stabbed them with stray graipe prongs,
who takes the penknife from Dad
to split the twine and toss liths
to calves and bullying cows in unlit lean-tos
as winter snows swirl through bare trees.

Goundwork

I

Sunday strollers chatter to each other
how bright the pillars are now they're painted,
gleaming fresh white in late July haze.

The wrought iron gates and capstones
also shine, bitumous black against
the hawthorn green and stubble gold.

Several times vandalism's been repaired;
each brushstroke dispels cracks, replastering,
missing spars, rust's amber stains.

II

I'd lean against the wooden strainers'
clasped arms, the tinsheet curve

of the head slipping round thorn bark,
sweat dripping from forehead onto specs

as you'd hammer a staple, amber sap
oozing from the wound like the blood globs

on the backs of hands scratched criss-cross
by barbs, thorns dark under the skin;

strand of wire vibrating under tension
mimicking the breath flexing your shirt.

III

The dusty aroma of teaded hay
wafts to the gateway's umber pad
dried to cracks where once pocks

of rain-filled muck sucked boots.
Who might dream tall sunflowers
may be rivalled by rosy-blooming henbit,

rude yellow ribwort,
bitter, white-capped ground elder,
by the pillar, feverfew's daisy-heads,

bindweed's creamy-pink blooms,
spindly horsetail, clumps of rosebay's
purple tears in bare soil patches.

IV
The dark purple blotch on your lobe
is benign, but your neck's red rash
will sting even if you rub it with docken.
Your brother once swung at you with this
billhook in fear of imaginary tormentors.
The sudden gasp of air that tosses
a patch of sward astray like a ghost
kicking his way through the crop
tickles your ear as the swish of that stroke
once did. You pullstart the chainsaw
and are anointed with confetti flakes, rasp
through stubborn boughs, stand aside
as each one totters precariously, tidy up
the lane-sides until it's time for home.

Pallet

He pauses to enter 'the zone', heaves,
the pallet rises from grasping thorn branches,
rolls on grass, before toppling flat;
he straddles barbed wire at the strainer post,
breathes heavily when he thuds onto earth.
Arms wide, fingers clenched on boards,
its weight on his shoulders, against his head,
he follows the blur of the dog's path.

Dark, now, when he gets in, removes boots
in the steamy-windowed back scullery.
The old fellow's nursing the teapot, shuffling
in slippers to the table, neck bent
as if he'd a hump; who listens jealously
to the report on the hedge hole patching.

Honest Ulsterman

(i.m. Jim Hewitt)

So you got away, then, Jim Hewitt;
over eighty years in this vale of tears
at an end. When I got to know you
you were already grey and stooped,
racked with pains in joints and wasted
muscles; seventy-three, you joined
sixty-something John and teenaged me
in his Wee Meadow to bend knees
and trail arms like flat-capped apes
scouring moist, acidic soil and clay
for spuds. Rain or hail, noses dripping,
we'd step gradually along each drill
as patient as a procession of clergy.
Blister-hardened fingers would hoke
past sharp stone edges to pluck each
tuber from its root-tangle; clinging
muck was rubbed off, so each potato
shone as bright as our eyes surveying
our latest, golden treasure trove find.
John would drive the put-put pre-War
Porsche tractor gingerly across ruts –
bonnet an avante garde moulding of
wrought-lifetime rust. You and I'd
sit on the back, legs dangling, shaking
from side to side, occasionally thrown
up by a sudden wheel-jerk to smack
hard on the wooden trailer boards
so that it'd make bottoms numb.
Agnes would have tea and a plate
of floury spuds ready on the range;
we'd sit at the table in the bay window,
looking out across a concrete expanse

to a courtyard of outhouses framed
by corrugated zinc roofs where
an ever unseen dog woofed. Butter melting
on the spuds, salt grains dissolving,
teacups clattering as we stirred milk in,
that's how I learned of your working
years, from leaving school at fourteen
till the machinery came, in the quarry.
All shovel and pick then – bicycle there
and home again – these guys th'day
that slabber about being tight men
wouldn't last a week at it. You spent
years, grey dust on scuffed boots and
trouser ends, grime under fingernails
and in the pores of your hands, polished
by the constant twist of flesh against wood,
shafts scouring as you spaded at trucks.
Always the grate of gravel agin' steel.
Yet you were a gentle man, taken aback
the day one fella lost the bap with
a mate and decked him a slug on the jaw.
You'd scarcely seen the like of it –
aye, there'd been the War, but all that
was worlds away in France or on newsreels.
Aye, there'd be riots in the town,
Cath'lics and Prods at each other's throats
'bout the shipyard, lobbing tram set-squares
at yin another lads th'day could barely lift,
but that was rare, maybe only Twelfth craic.
Folk like you, Jim, just kept your heads
down at your work like God-fearing buddies,
paid no heed to sectarian squabbles
when you'd a family to rear and rent
to stump up. You never cursed, never
blasphemed, never spoke bad of anyone,
got on with your lot without complaint.

And now you've got away, Jim Hewitt;
wherever you've gone, it's a better place
for having you in it – as my world's been,
my life's been, due to your brief presence.

Groundkeepers

('Eliminate groundkeepers, as they harbour disease',
Dept. of Agriculture advice brochure)

Thon wee ones, Da called them; referring
to family lore, those who survived the famine
by secreting these tiny *prutas* in pockets.
Ammunition. Seed that would see them through the
    worst.
My patch of potatoes cannot match their struggle.
And when I turn up tuber specks but
don't salvage, chuck them with the waste, in my stomach
there stalks an ancient hunger.

Genetic Engineering

The spade whoks through damp earth,
brown powder spills as I root
for gold nuggets: tubers clutched
together like a nest of eggs secreted
by some sharp-eyed reptile that'll dart
forth snapping. Not that a parent knows the worth
of its offspring: some are weak, most ordinary,
finding a prodigy, there's the rarity.

Jack warned it can take a decade to breed
a viable variety, a lifetime to produce
a *pruta* like this, with near-perfect characteristics;
but I didn't follow the man's strain when he said,
good berries may not trip the spud fantastic
but bad seed never made anything of any use.

On An Onion

On the surface you were flaky, would shed dry skin
when touched, rust-like matter betrayed where hands had been.
I tried to reach your core, began peeling; layer
after layer, first smooth, green veined, before paler
strata gave way to translucence. And as I peeled,
and mysterious realities were revealed,
my eyes smarted, tears welled as I blinked back the pain
of rupturing the essence of a spring onion.

Your aphrodisiac qualities worked on me:
boiling, the tart aroma tickled my fancy;
spread before me, I feasted on your tender flesh,
lost in the ecstasy of succulence, the clash
of flavours – your circumscribed firmness and freshness
opposed to the milder korma's licit caress.

A Farmhouse Kitchen
In County Antrim

If I should dare to speak of a home
that lacks certain contemporary glitz
it's not because I mean to cock-a-snook,
there's a definite mystique about the kitchen
of a farmhouse that's seen Troubles and Blitz
come and go and not lost its distinctiveness.
There may be a new sink-unit, wallpaper,
curtains, paint, but the floor tiles,
the shape and style of this room remain.
A dimness pervades ceiling corners
despite the deep-silled bay-windows; the doors
retain Edwardian knobs and locks;
the range radiates by worn-armed chairs
covered with musty, pastel fabrics.
But the unique character conveyed
resides not merely in an inventory
of furniture or artefacts, bric-a-brac
or décor. A sullen grandeur adheres to
the humanity dwelling within these walls.
Those years of toil, decades of hardship
the trials of family wiles, fortune's lot,
conjugate to create more than just
a trip down memory lane: the stoic
resilience of their tranquillity has taught me
a greater truth than textbook, pulpit,
lectern, court bench, lamppost, pillowcase.
If I could live as they have lived,
in serene good faith and, despite all pride
or anguish, dispose enough detachment
to still discover as sublime and wonder at
nature's symmetry, then perhaps I'd be

at-one with what really matters, have gained
at last an inkling of the peace something
within craves as my preferred destiny.

The Unrequited

A van choking to a halt on a back-road,
amidst dreeping, overarching hedges;
the lad cowers under a coat, slurries
to the farmhouse where one dim light signals
charity. The old boy carries tools for him,
holds a torch as he delves beneath the bonnet;
startles like a rabbit at his fierce eyes.

Kids, hands in pockets, snigger as he pays
for fuel at the counter: cheeks flush pink,
imagining the stranger, later, stopping here,
telling about the fruit who stroked his thigh.
Surely the whole country knows: how he risked
rejection. Within the year, he's left all to the church.

The Accordionists

My father-in-law gigged at Carnegie Hall,
my father ceilied in Loanends Orange Hall.

On the living room wall, with Pat Boone in cowboy hat,
alongside President McAleese, a bronze accordionist.

A video captures Paddy's Galloglass arrangements,
Late Late Show footage, trad. entertainment.

Dad's mate upturned a tea-chest as drums,
stour rose to their rustic thrums;

the youth of Ireland, in more innocent times,
North and South romanced to self-taught rhythms.

When confirming bookings for each night,
'no ham' was the main clause Sheila'd write.

Elder

Some might stereotype your kind
as emblematic of a time
when discrimination cast you lucky,
them not. Yet even if you reaped
benefits because of the twist of fate
that meant you were born
into our society's higher caste,
there's no evidence
that you conspired or shared
in others' bigotry.
You weren't active in supporting
the oppressed; does that make you complicit
in oppression? A sin of omission...
So many of us are guilty of that
type of sin in so many scenarios.
Some, so blinded by their bitterness,
view you among the bigots -
this gentle man, who stood in the vestibule
of your church each Sunday morning,
bored adults and kids alike
with parochial nosiness.
I recall you stepping reverently
along the aisle's deep blue carpet
with the wooden offering plate,
head bowed, twinkle in your eye
as you acknowledged friends
with a nod, the firm press of your hand
as we crowded from each service
as if parting for the last time.

The Latest Crisis

(i.m. Robert Gray)

You walked slowly from the park to your car,
as old men do; I don't know who found you there
slumped over the wheel, bald pate
unselfconsciously on display. Were you late
home, did someone phone, or did someone
notice? call for help? – which you were beyond.
The afternoon paper beside you, headlines
trumpeting the latest political despond.
As if any crisis could be greater than the loss
of a neighbour as good as this.

Missing The Mark

I should been revising for exams,
instead, I chucked arrows at the board
on the back of a sister's bedroom door,
a drooping poster of Ophelia – Lucifer
in gothic drag – swooning
as darts disturbed target segments.
Soon, the distraction of charms:
floosies at the pub after a hard day's graft,
the hope that this time the fruit machine pays.

Elegy For The Black Hill

Driving over the resurfaced
stretch of road, I stab off the rock CD.
Following the turn of the motorway
a quick cast of a cold eye reminds me that
bulldozers have peeled off turf the way
Hong Kong restaurateurs will skin a live snake.
Dumper trucks have carted soil away.
The triangulation pillar's gone.
The summit of the Black Hill is disappearing
into a pit. Diggers strike.
Millennia of strata will be crushed to supply
the hunger for hardcore. I strain to catch a glimpse
of brown stain on skyline.

Last Evening

(i.m. Robert Coulter)

There's a chill this summer evening
as you're leaning on the gate, draw
on a fag, bark at the clawing
pup that snuffs in soil
while flowerheads chug and dark
cloud above the hill casts
a trail of fluff above
this patchwork valley's masts
and trees. The cigarette tip
blazes scarlet when you suck,
taking a long, indulgent
draft, a nostalgia trip
beyond articulation's arc.
The acrid smog drifts
with dew-mown grass's aroma.
Your granddaughter is cooing, squatting
in a sandpit, spading, patting
an entire world of roads,
houses, factories, plus temple.
She's your namesake; has inherited
your curly locks and dreadful wit.
You tell me your sister is to visit
tomorrow; the first time
you'll have met in a long while;
and as the low sun blinds
our eyes with its distracting glow
your lips form a smile;
as if acknowledging some kind
of resolution or mutual forgiveness.

Vision

(i.m. John McGrath)

Strains of *Be Thou My Vision* commence
as your coffin is wheeled into the hall
of the funeral parlour.
A few days hence, I wheeled your latest grandson,
a few days old, into the sitting room
and you slipped a score in the sleeping child's pram.
As we bow our heads to pray
you'd have a wry smile
at the spider scurrying on the wall
and skirting board, like a louse on a hat.
The spider's so busy she's a blur –
like your father in that photo they called him
from ploughing to take, because sisters
were visiting from the States.
You would approve of this insect's disregard
for social niceties, her preference
for getting things done -
none of this fruitless speculation,
interminably seeking the kernel,
as we follow you on your final journey -
floating to the centre on a flimsy thread.

Return To The Hill

Winter's lasted a year -
nothing but cloud and cold,
brittleness, rot, loss.
But jumpleads start the tractor.
It idles as he cuts cord
to remove gates and fences
that divided this field
while the pipeline was forced across.
Twine slackens in his hand,
Jacob's ladder breaks through,
the gate falls aside as he rises
from his knees, feels warmth
on his face, turns to witness
light transfiguring river and bough.